Patterns Two

I0465735

Patterns Two
Copyright © 2018 by Dave Reed

All of these designs were taken from Public Domain sources. The author reworked them to create derivative works which are now protected by copyright.

You may photocopy a few pages and redistribute those, but you may not market them for profit without permission from the author.

All rights reserved under International and Pan-American Copyright Conventions.

ISBN: 9781790431229

Designed by Dave Reed

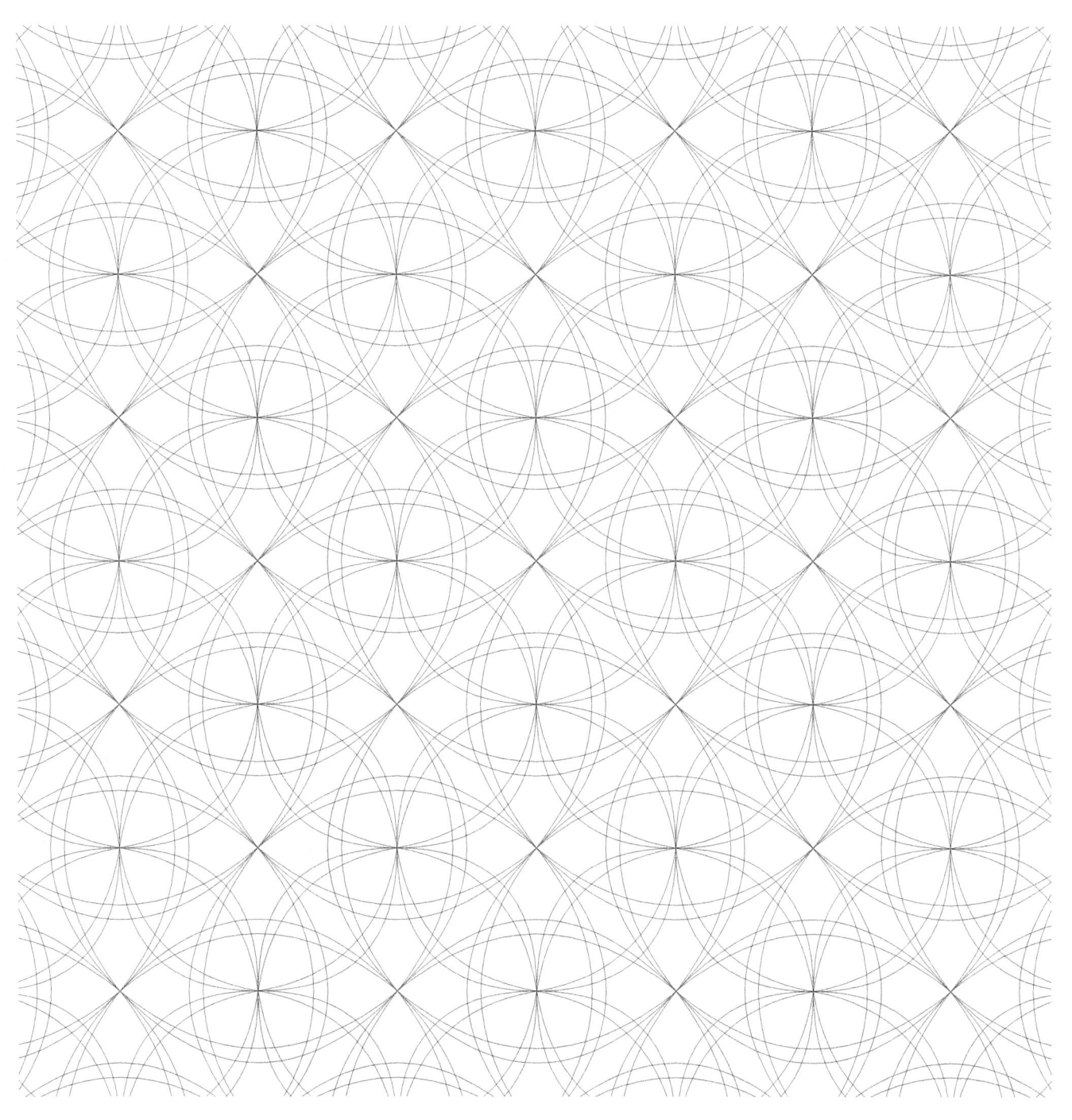

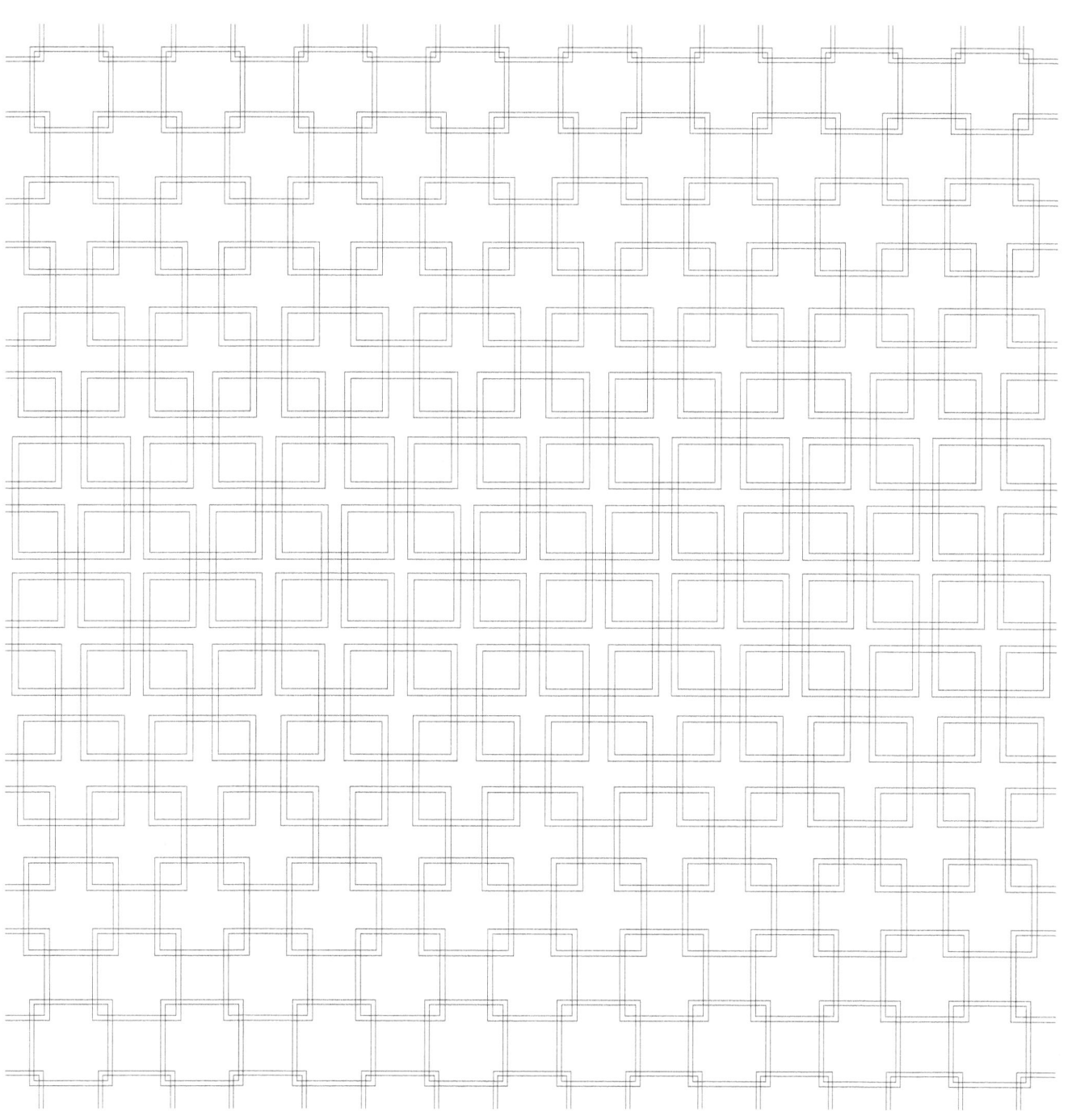

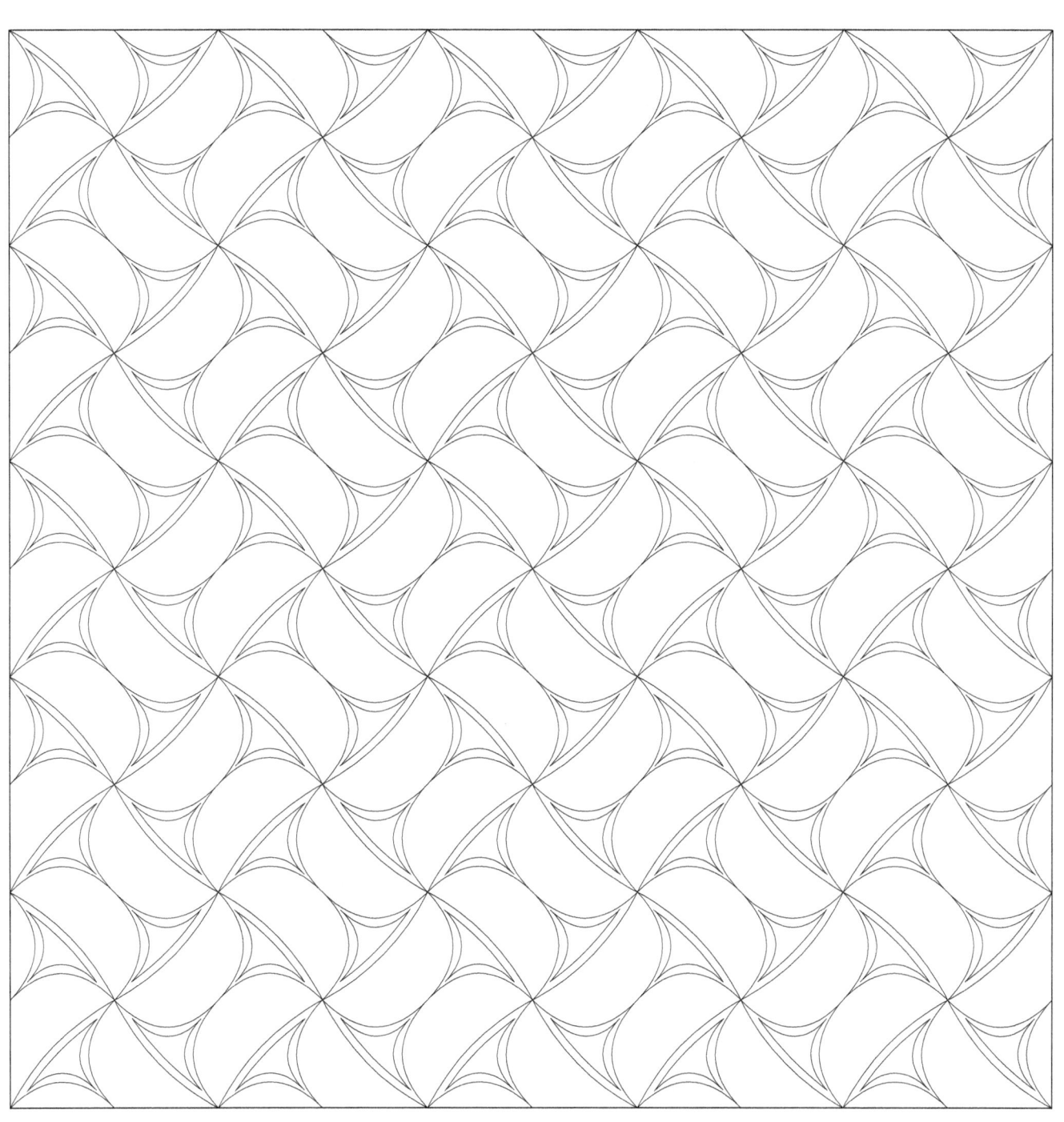

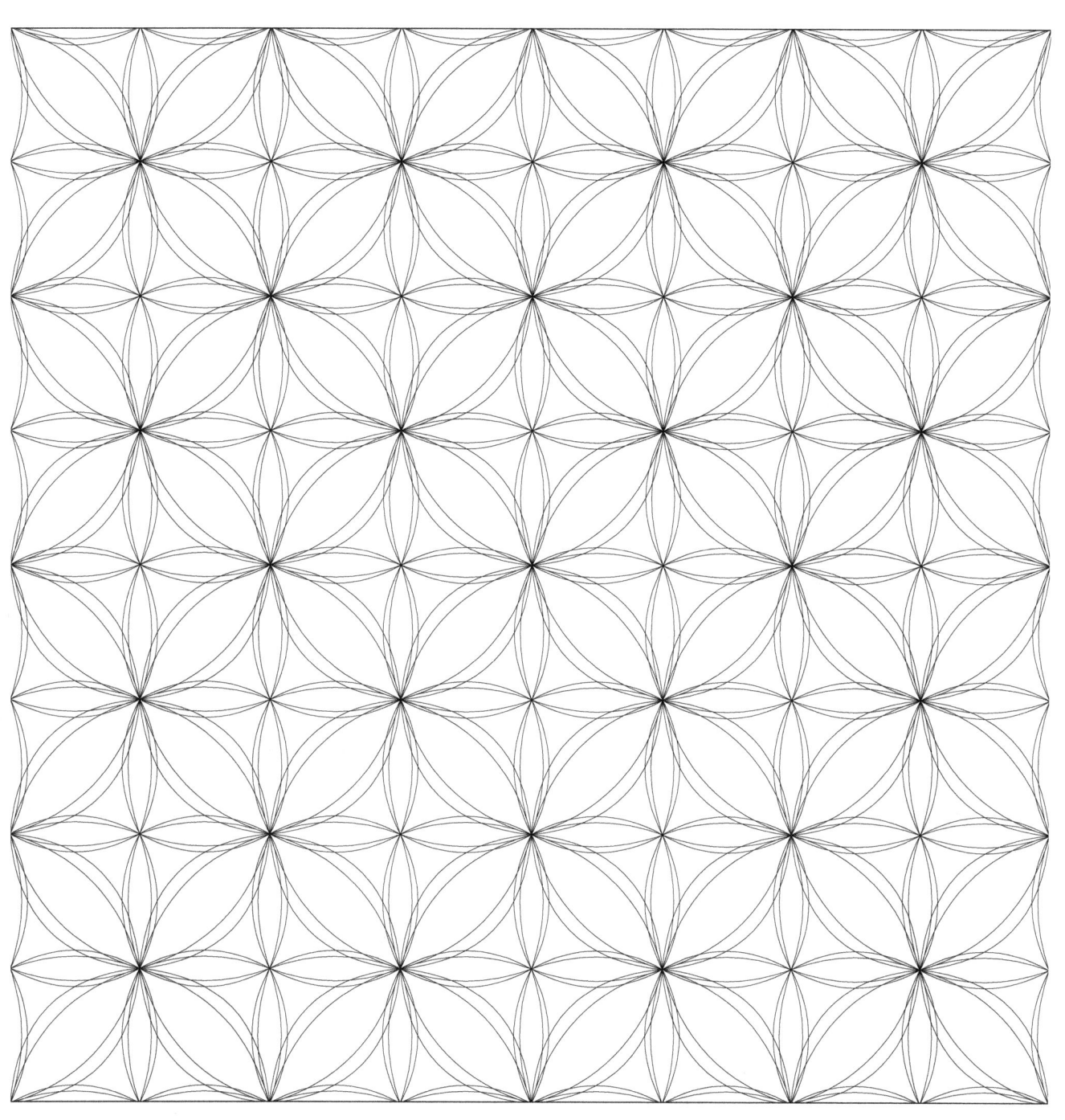

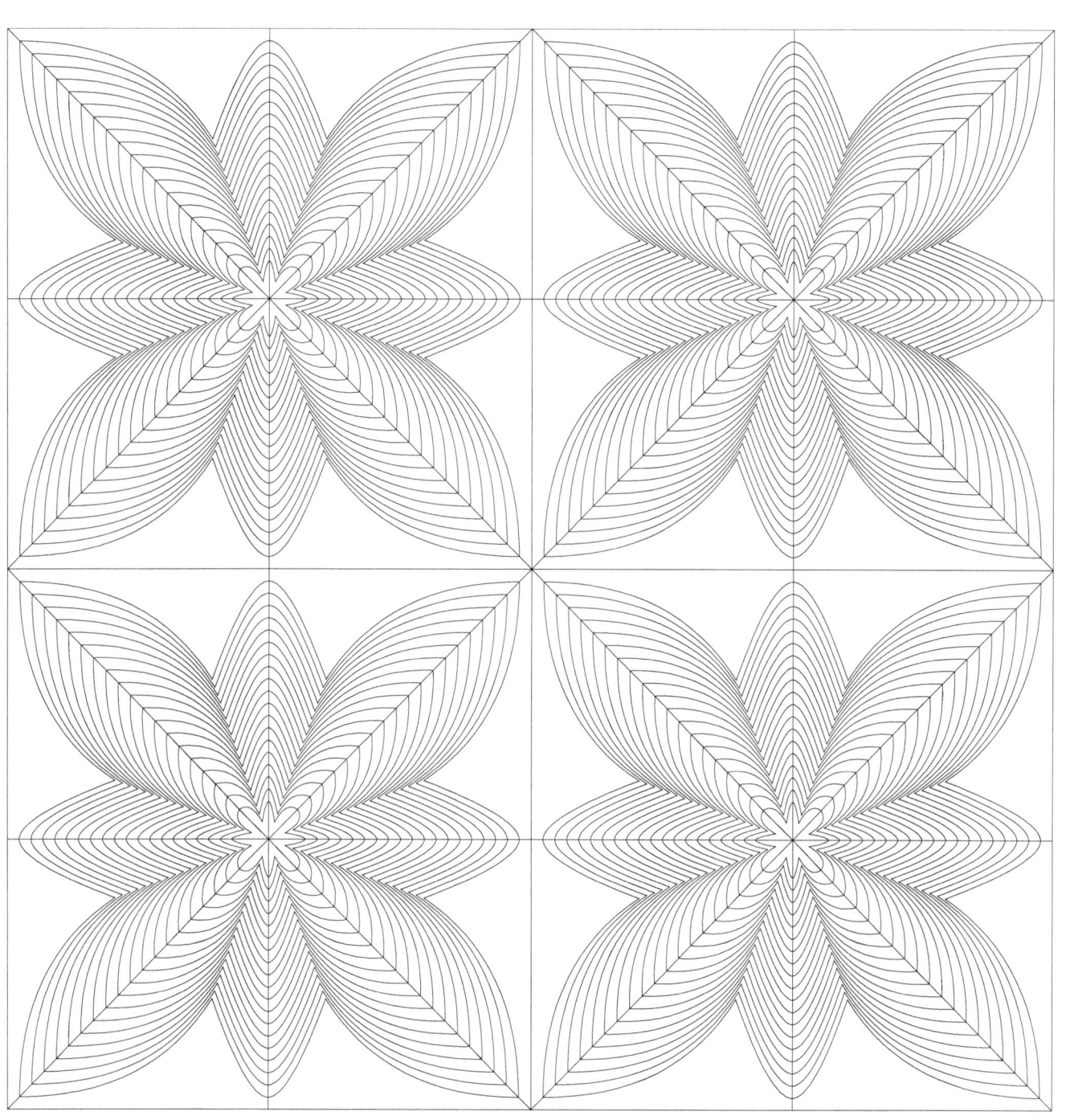

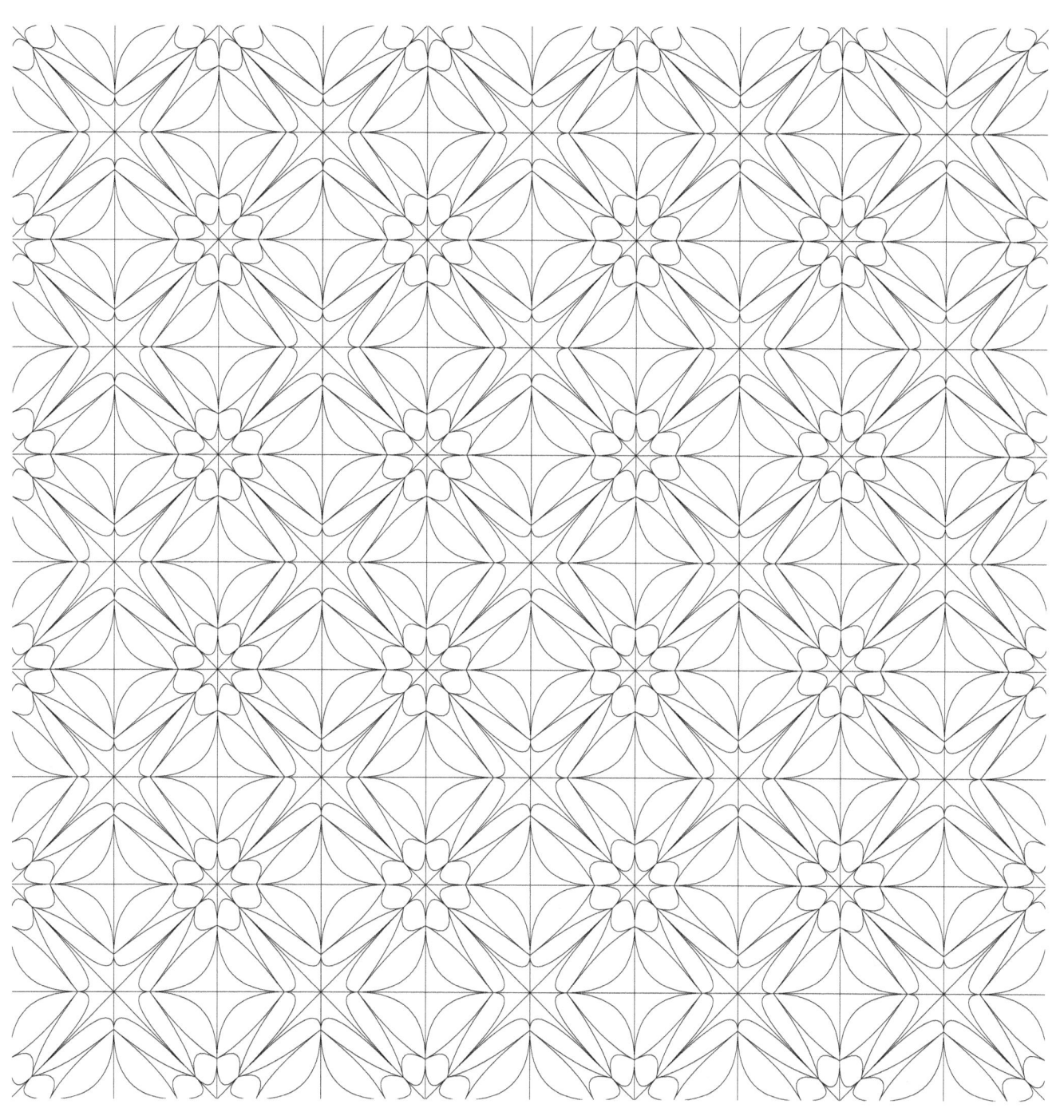

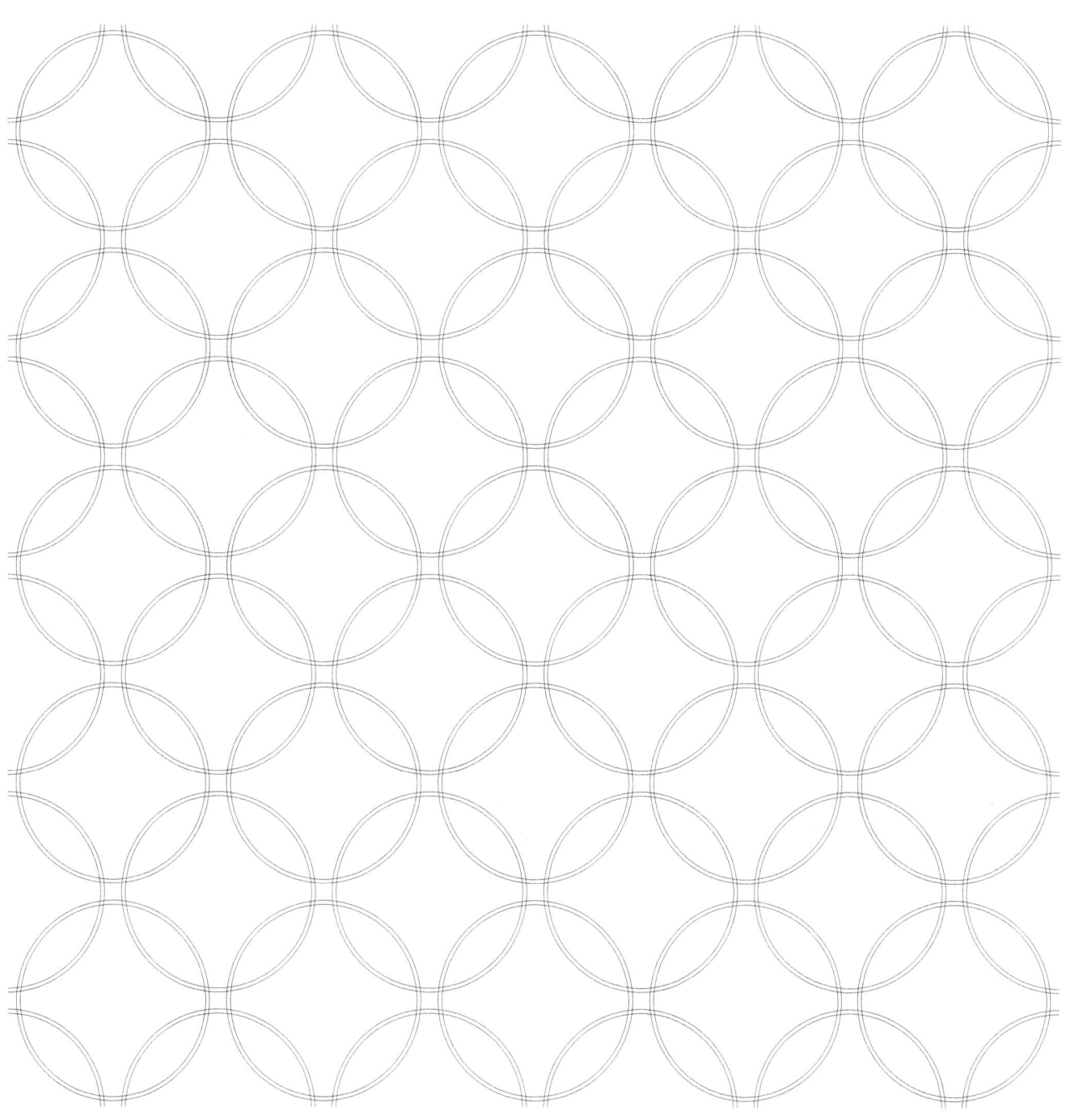

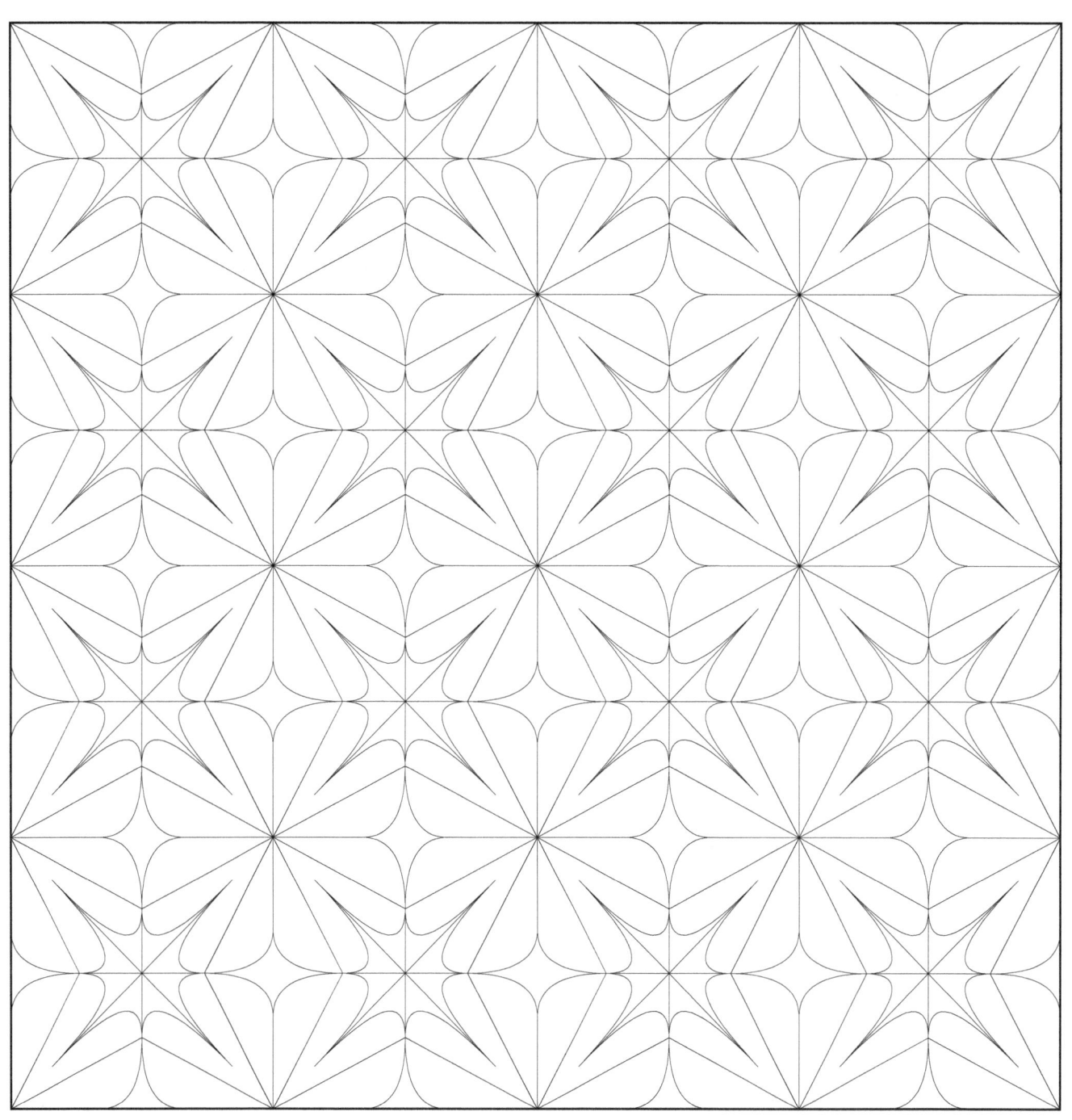

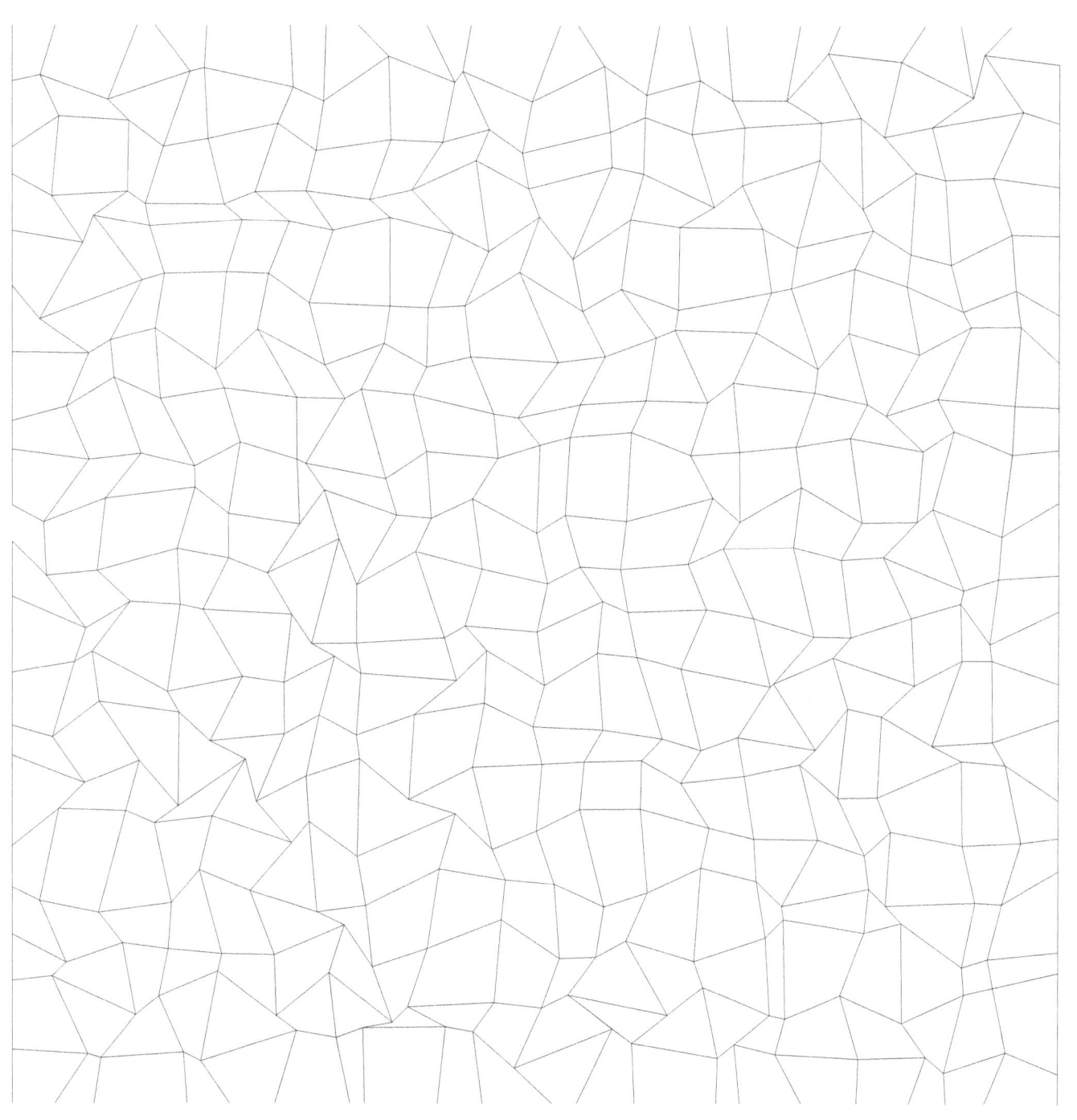

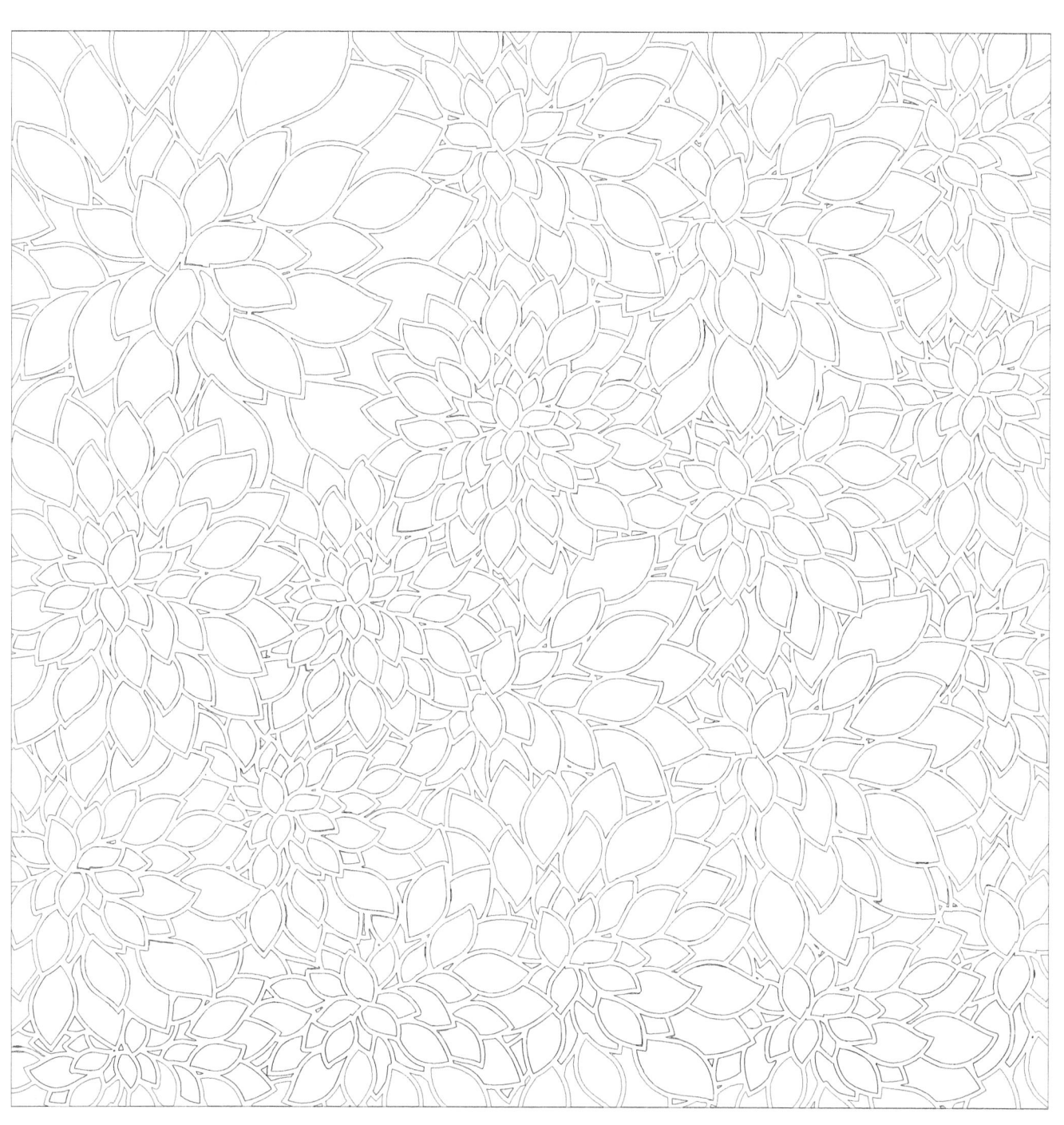

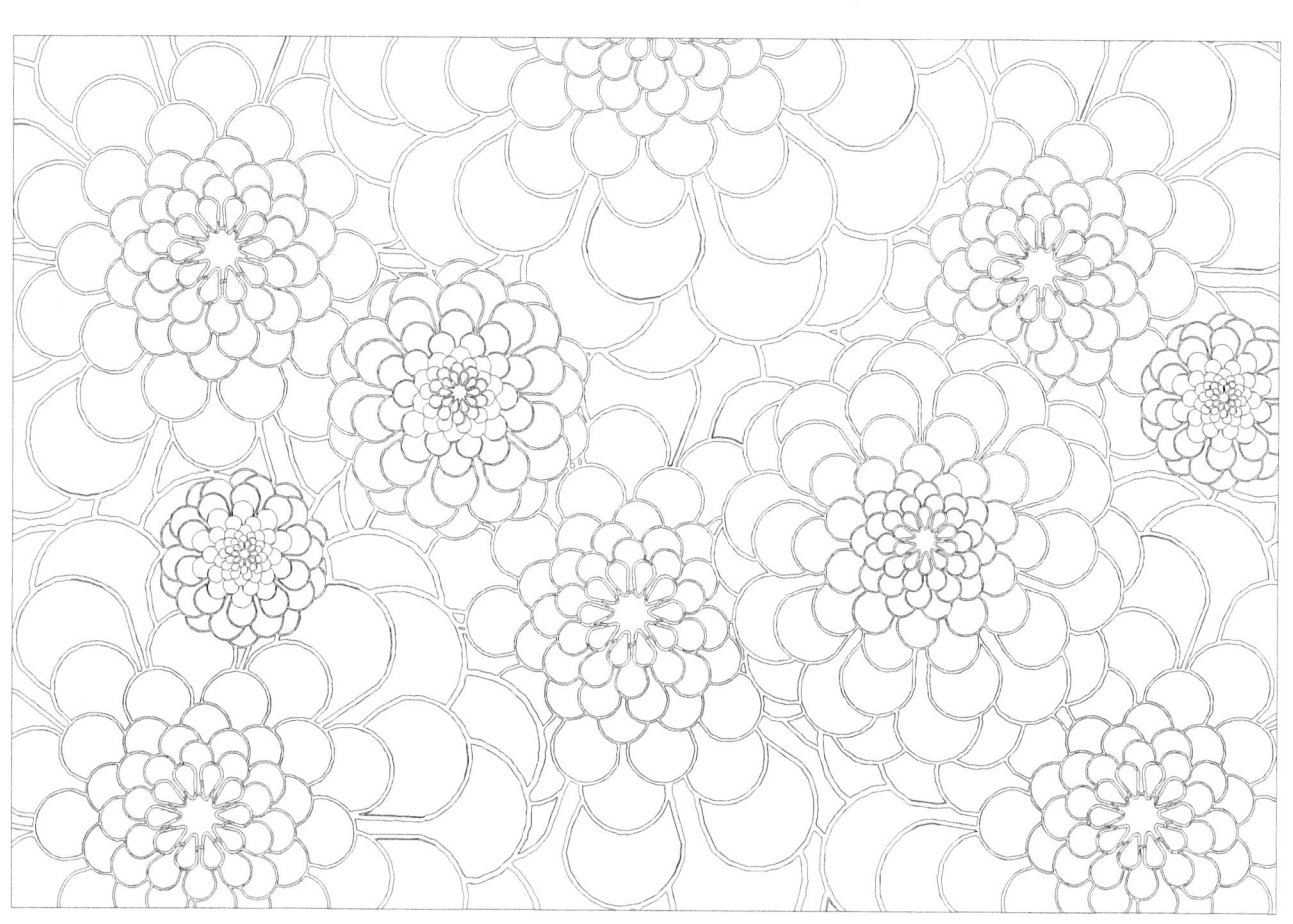

www.ingramcontent.com/pod-product-compliance
Lightning Source LLC
Chambersburg PA
CBHW081551220526
45468CB00014B/2916